P9-CQZ-305

SCHOOLS OF THE SACRED HEART
HOFFMAN LIBRARY
2222 Broadway
San Francisco, CA 94115
415-292-3156

LOOKING AT THE INTERDEPENDENCE OF PLANTS, ANIMALS, AND THE ENVIRONMENT WITH GRAPHIC ORGANIZERS

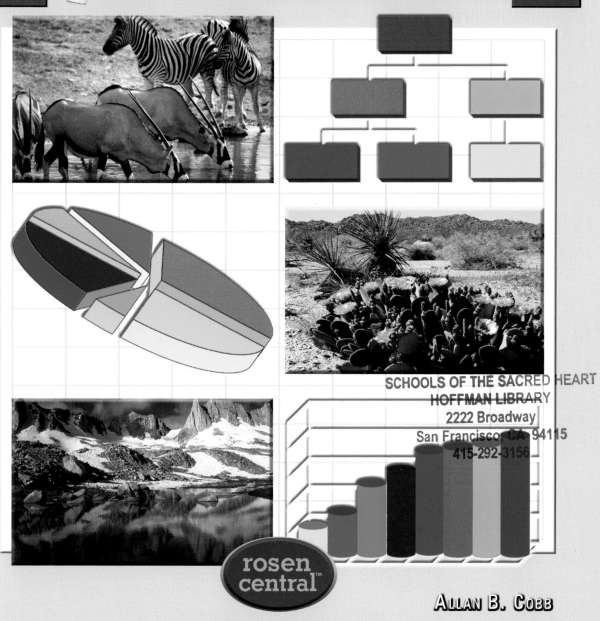

SCHOOLS OF THE SACRED HEART
HOFFMAN LIBRARY
2222 Broadway
San Francisco, CA 94115
415-292-3156

rosen
central™

ALLAN B. COBB

The Rosen Publishing Group, Inc., New York

Published in 2006 by The Rosen Publishing Group, Inc.
29 East 21st Street, New York, NY 10010

Copyright © 2006 by The Rosen Publishing Group, Inc.

First Edition

All rights reserved. No part of this book may be reproduced in any form without permission in writing from the publisher, except by a reviewer.

Library of Congress Cataloging-in-Publication Data

Cobb, Allan B.
Looking at the interdependence of plants, animals, and the environment with graphic organizers/Allan B. Cobb.
    p. cm.—(Using graphic organizers to study the living environment)
Includes bibliographical references and index.
ISBN 1-4042-0615-9 (lib. bdg.)
1. Ecology—Juvenile literature. 2. Ecology—Study and teaching (Elementary)—Graphic methods.
I. Title. II. Series.
QH541.14.C61 2005
577—dc22

                                                      2005017629

Manufactured in the United States of America

On the cover: A bar chart *(top right)*, a pie chart *(center)*, and a flow chart *(bottom left)*.

CONTENTS

INTRODUCTION

Plants and animals depend on each other to survive. Plants use sunlight to make food and take in carbon dioxide and release oxygen. Animals need both food and oxygen to survive. In return, animals help plants by providing resources for plants. Some animals even pollinate plants so the plants can reproduce. Plants and animals are also dependent on the environment. Each plant and animal has specific requirements from the environment. For example, some plants need soil that holds water while other plants need soil that stays dry. Some animals, such as cows, eat and digest grasses, while deer mainly eat leafy plants because they do not digest grass well. Each plant and animal is adapted to its environment. It is for this reason that polar bears are not found in the tropics and redwood trees are not found at the North Pole. They are each best suited for where they live and likely couldn't survive elsewhere.

Sometimes the relationships that form among plants, animals, and the environment are direct while at other times they are not. These relationships include animals feeding on plants, plants getting

Plants, animals, and the environment, which include these deer, polar bears, and redwood trees, are all interdependent on one another.

nutrients from the soil, and animals transporting plant seeds from one place to another. Scientists spend years studying these relationships to understand how they affect each other. New relationships are being discovered all the time. These relationships are often very complex. Sometimes scientists discover that seemingly unrelated actions in one part of the environment have a drastic effect on a plant or animal in another part of the environment. Scientists still do not fully understand all the connections among plants, animals, and the environment.

This book is an introduction to some of these connections. To help you understand some of the complex concepts presented here, graphic organizers are used. Graphic organizers help you to understand information by organizing the data so it may be interpreted visually. Sometimes while reading, it is difficult to follow complex connections and see how they relate. Graphic organizers help by illustrating the connections.

CHAPTER ONE

PRINCIPLES OF ECOLOGY

Every organism is connected in some way to many other organisms. Some plants depend on other plants for a place to live. For example, most trees need lots of sunlight. This is one of the reasons that trees grow tall, to reach the sunlight in dense forests. Other plants cannot tolerate much sunlight and actually need shade. These types of plants are often found growing in the shade of trees. The tree gets lots of sunlight but also provides shade for the other plants. Some plants depend on particular insects to pollinate their flowers. Some animals depend on plants for food. Some animals depend on other animals for food. Most fungi depend on dead plants and animals for food. Sometimes these connections are obvious, like a bee pollinating a flower, and other times these are not so obvious, such as a tree providing shade for other plants.

Every organism also depends on the environment. The environment is more than just a place to live; it provides moisture, nutrients, and oxygen. Without the environment, neither plants nor animals could survive.

Different types of plants have different requirements for survival. Most grasses need a lot of sunlight and are usually found growing in open fields where sunlight is abundant.

WHAT IS ECOLOGY?

The branch of science that studies the interactions and interdependence among plants, animals, and the environment is called ecology. Ecology reveals the relationships between the living and nonliving parts of the environment. Ecologists gather information from many different fields, including botany (the science of plants), zoology (the

ECOLOGY VENN DIAGRAM

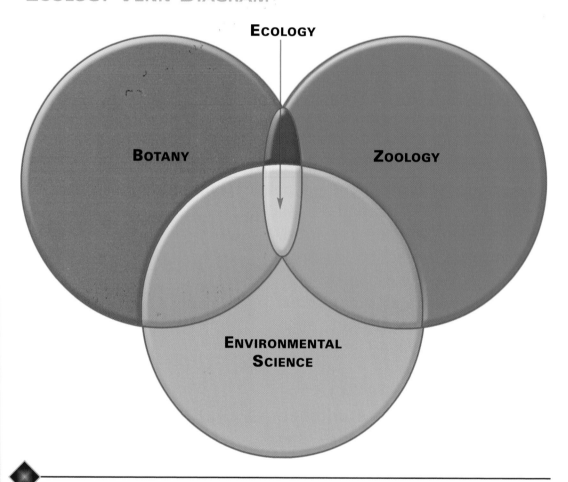

Venn diagrams are designed to illustrate several different subjects and what they have in common, which is represented by the overlap of their circles. As this Venn diagram shows, ecology is composed of a mixture of different subjects, including botany, zoology, and environmental science.

science of animals), environmental science, geology (the science of rocks and the history of the earth), chemistry, and physics.

The environment is made up of two parts—the biotic and the abiotic. Biotic factors include all the organisms: plants, animals, protists, fungi, and bacteria. Abiotic factors include all the nonliving parts of the environment. Abiotic factors are things such as wind, precipitation, humidity, temperature, light, air, and soil. The abiotic factors can have a direct effect on the biotic factors in the environment. For

IDEA RAKE

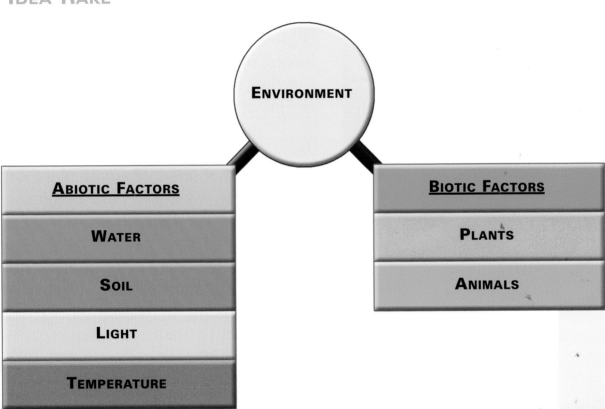

An idea rake illustrates a concept and divides it into its component parts. As this idea rake shows, there are many variables that affect the environment, including those from both nonliving (abiotic) and living (biotic) things.

ORGANISM

POPULATION

COMMUNITY

ECOSYSTEM

BIOSPHERE

example, a drought could cause plants to wither and die, thus taking away a food source for animals.

LEVELS OF ORGANIZATION

The study of the interdependence of plants, animals, and the environment can take place on many different levels of organization. Studying these levels of organizations can reveal relationships between organisms and their environments. Depending on the level of organization that is studied, this information may apply to a single organism, a group of organisms, or even many groups of different organisms.

The most basic level of organization is the individual organism. This can be either an individual plant or animal. For example, an ecologist may study a single male alligator. The study will tell much about what that alligator eats, when it is active and when it is sleeping, how it moves, and its breeding behavior.

The next broadest level of organization is a population. A population is

Level of organization ladders help us to visualize the hierarchy of a system. This ladder shows that at the top, the organism is the highest level of organization in an ecosystem. The lowest level is the biosphere.

Sea lions move awkwardly on land, so they depend on each other for protection by staying in large groups. Some members of the group watch for predators or other signs of danger.

a group of organisms of a single species that lives and interbreeds in the same location at the same time. An ecologist studying a population of alligators might look at population growth rates, the effect of the population on the environment, or predict changes in population size.

The next level of organization is the community. A community is a collection of populations that interact with each other. An ecologist studying a community might look at how adding or removing a species affects all the different populations, how resources are divided among the populations, or how changes in size in one population affect the other populations.

After the community, the ecosystem is the next broadest level of organization. As mentioned earlier, an ecosystem is made up of the interactions among the populations in a community and the abiotic factors in the environment. Terrestrial ecosystems are those found on land such as forests, grasslands, and deserts. Aquatic ecosystems are those in either fresh or salt water. Freshwater ecosystems include streams, ponds, and lakes. Saltwater or marine ecosystems are found in the oceans. An ecologist who studies ecosystems might look at the abiotic or biotic factors that keep the various communities stable or how changes in those factors make the communities unstable.

The broadest level of organization is the biosphere. The biosphere is made up of the entire area of the planet where life exists. This extends from the depths of the oceans and deep underground to very high in the atmosphere. It includes all the biotic and abiotic factors on the planet. At this level of organization, an ecologist would be concerned with all interactions that take place among the ecosystems and the planet.

Some very large animals, such as this caribou, depend on very small plants, such as mosses, for food. During the summer, these animals eat large amounts of plant life to help build body fat for energy to survive through the winter.

HOW ORGANISMS INTERACT

The most important way that organisms interact is through their feeding behaviors. Energy is an important resource for organisms. Plants are unique because they convert energy from sunlight, carbon dioxide, and water into glucose. Glucose is an energy molecule that can be used by both plants and animals. Organisms break the chemical bonds in the glucose for energy. Because plants use energy from sunlight to make food, they are called autotrophs. Organisms that depend on autotrophs for their energy are called heterotrophs.

Organisms are classified by the way they obtain their energy. Plants are considered producers because they produce their own energy using sunlight. Animals cannot produce their own energy so they must consume their energy. For this reason, animals are called consumers. Animals that eat only plants are called herbivores, such as cows and deer. Animals that eat other animals are called carnivores. Animals that eat both plants and animals are called omnivores.

Some animals that are carnivores do not kill their own food. These animals find the remains of animals that have already died or been killed and they eat them. These animals are called scavengers. Some organisms, such as fungi, break down and consume nutrients from dead plant and animal matter. These organisms are called decomposers. Scavengers and decomposers both have

OBSERVATION CHART

COMMENSALISM	MUTUALISM	PARASITISM

Observation charts visually organize subjects into vertical columns. At the top of each column is the subject name. Below it is either a description or a visual representation of the subject. This observation chart illustrates the three different types of relationships between organisms: commensalism, mutualism, and parasitism.

important roles in the ecosystem. Scavengers remove dead animals from the ecosystem to keep them from building up. Decomposers break down dead plants and animals and assist in recycling the nutrients through the environment.

INTERDEPENDENCE AMONG ORGANISMS

At one time, biologists believed that all organisms competed with each other for survival. When biologists began exploring and studying the relationships among different organisms, they found that not all organisms compete. In some cases, organisms of different species have interdependent relationships. One of the most obvious is the predator-prey relationship. The predator is the hunter. It catches and eats other animals. The animals it eats are called prey.

Plants and animals also have other kinds of specialized relationships. A symbiotic relationship is a close one between organisms of different species. There are several different kinds of symbiotic relationships that exist among organisms. Commensalism is a symbiotic relationship in which one species benefits and the other species is neither harmed nor helped. Mutualism is a symbiotic relationship in which both species benefit from the relationship. Parasitism is a symbiotic relationship in which one species benefits while the other species is harmed.

It is important for scientists to define the role of an organism in the environment. Once an organism's role is defined, scientists can compare it to organisms with similar roles in different ecosystems. This gives scientists an understanding of how organisms adapt to different conditions and how they depend on other organisms.

Chapter Two

Ecosystems

All organisms get their energy by breaking down chemical bonds in food molecules. Plants produce their own energy by capturing the energy in sunlight and using it to convert water and carbon dioxide into glucose. The glucose molecule stores energy in the chemical bonds of glucose. Animals cannot make their own energy molecules, so they must consume them by eating other organisms. For example, when a cow eats grass, it is eating the matter in the grass. As the cow digests the grass, the matter is broken down into energy and nutrients. The cow uses the energy and absorbs the nutrients into its body. Some of the energy is used to maintain all the functions of the cow's body while the excess energy is stored as fat. When one organism eats another organism, both matter and energy are passed from one organism to another.

Ecologists describe the passing of matter and energy from one organism to the next as a food chain. A food chain is a simple model that shows how matter and energy move through an ecosystem. The food chain graphic organizer on the next page shows a simple food chain that exists in a pond. Algae are autotrophs because they produce their own energy from sunlight. When a minnow eats algae, it uses the energy stored in the algae—matter in the form of other nutrients and minerals—as an energy source. The minnow uses the algae's stored energy to help it grow. When the sunfish eats the minnow, it uses the energy and matter that was stored in the minnow. Finally, when the bass eats the sunfish, it uses the matter and energy from the sunfish. A food chain simply illustrates how matter and energy are passed from one organism to the next.

A food chain is a very simple representation of matter and energy transfer. These matter and energy transfers are much more complex when an ecologist actually studies them. For example, a sunfish may not be the only organism in a pond that eats minnows. When all the organisms in a pond are added, the interdependence of all the organisms becomes much clearer. This type of a diagram is called a food web. A food web is a diagram that shows all the possible feeding relationships in the entire community.

FOOD CHAIN

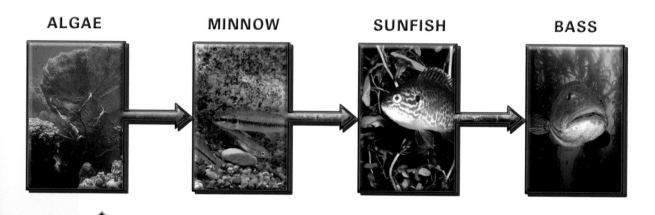

ALGAE **MINNOW** **SUNFISH** **BASS**

A food chain shows how energy and matter move from one organism to another. The direction of the arrows shows the direction the energy and matter flow. First, the minnow feeds on the algae. The sunfish then feeds on the minnow. Finally, the bass feeds on the sunfish.

A food web is also a good model to show how matter and energy pass through different organisms. It illustrates the complex nature of interdependence among plants and animals. Ecologists can use a food web to predict what will happen in an ecosystem when one species is increased in population size or completely removed. For example, in the pond ecosystem in the graphic

FOOD WEB

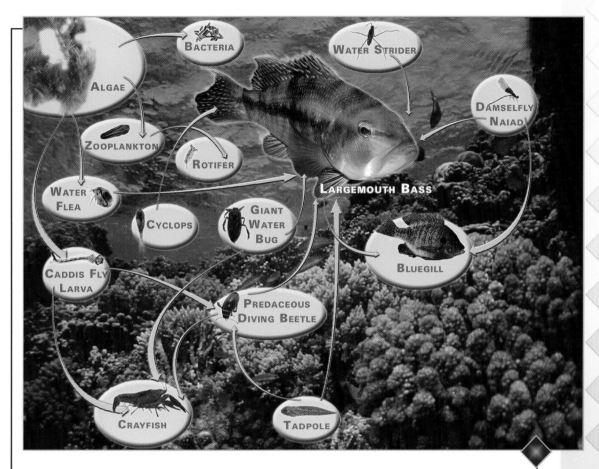

Food webs depict which organisms consume which in an ecosystem. In this food web, algae is eaten by bacteria, zooplankton, and water fleas, among other organisms. Those organisms are then eaten by others, such as crayfish and predaceous diving beetles. The primary consumer here is the largemouth bass.

organizer above, which organisms would be affected if minnows were removed from the ecosystem? How would it affect other populations if the population size of minnows doubled?

ENERGY AND TROPHIC LEVELS

Energy is one of the most important resources that is passed through an ecosystem. Almost all ecosystems depend on energy from the sun. Because animals cannot create their own energy, they depend on plants to produce energy. Plants absorb energy from the sun. When an animal eats plants, it gets the energy stored in the plant. When another animal eats that animal, it gets the energy from that animal.

In an ecosystem, plants are considered producers because they produce energy in a usable form. Because they produce more energy than they need, they store this energy. It is the stored energy that is available to the animal that eats the plants. This animal is called a primary consumer because it is eating a producer. An animal that eats other animals is called a secondary consumer because it is farther away from the original producer in the food chain. Tertiary consumers consume secondary consumers. Each of these levels—producer, primary consumer, secondary consumer, and tertiary consumer—is called a trophic level.

Trophic levels in an ecosystem are represented as a pyramid. The shape is a pyramid because there is less energy available to each trophic level from producers to secondary and tertiary consumers. The amount of energy that is transferred from one trophic level to the next is only about 10 percent. But what happens to the other 90 percent of the energy?

ENERGY PYRAMID

HAWKS

SNAKES

MICE

PLANTS

The pyramid is an excellent graphic organizer for illustrating hierarchies. This energy pyramid shows the amount of energy available at each trophic level. Plants provide the most amount of energy, being the most eaten. Hawks provide the least.

Every organism requires energy to carry out its life processes. That energy comes from food molecules. The process used by organisms to obtain energy from food molecules is called cellular respiration. One of the products of cellular respiration is heat. Heat is lost to the environment during the process. This heat loss accounts for the 90 percent of the energy lost at each trophic level.

Because only 10 percent of the available energy is passed up the trophic pyramid at each level, the number of organisms at each level is also reduced as you go higher up the pyramid. The pyramid cannot support more organisms at any level than the energy available from the trophic level below it. This is one of the factors that creates stable populations at each trophic level. When population changes occur, the result of those changes can cause changes throughout the entire trophic pyramid.

THE CARBON CYCLE

As you have seen, energy passes through an ecosystem by moving from one trophic level to another. Matter also passes through an ecosystem, but it cycles through it instead of passing through the ecosystem like energy. The types of matter that commonly cycle through an ecosystem are carbon, water, nitrogen, and phosphorus. All of these types of matter are very important to all living organisms.

Plants convert carbon dioxide (CO_2) from the atmosphere into organic carbon molecules. Plants take in carbon dioxide during photosynthesis and use it to build organic molecules. Plants combine carbon dioxide and water using energy from the sun to make glucose. Plants convert glucose into other compounds and store it for later use. When animals eat plants, they use the stored energy for food and to build tissues. This transfers carbon from plants to animals.

Carbon in the form of carbon dioxide is important for plants to make food. But how does carbon dioxide get into the atmosphere? Plants and animals break down carbon compounds during cellular respiration. This process releases both stored energy and carbon dioxide. This returns carbon dioxide to the atmosphere. Trees retain carbon in their wood. When this wood burns, the carbon is released as carbon dioxide. These are just two of many ways that carbon is returned to the atmosphere as carbon dioxide.

When plants and animals die, they decompose or break down. Decomposition releases carbon directly back into the atmosphere.

Sometimes the remains of plants or animals are buried quickly or decompose in swamps with low oxygen levels. When the remains are captured in the ground or in swamps in this way, the carbon is not immediately returned to the atmosphere. When this happens, the carbon may be locked away for thousands or millions of years.

CARBON CYCLE FLOW CHART

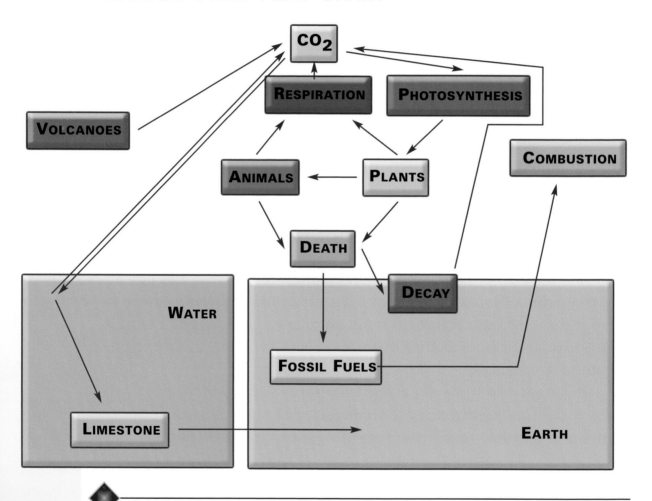

A flow chart shows the path of movement of a thing or idea. This flow chart illustrates the carbon cycle. As you can see, carbon is recycled throughout the environment by a number of means.

Geological processes, heat, and pressure may turn this trapped carbon into oil, coal, or natural gas. Because these forms of carbon are tied up for long periods of time, they are called fossil fuels. When people burn these fossil fuels for energy, the carbon is released back into the atmosphere as carbon dioxide.

When animals die, the carbon in their bodies is either passed to another animal, or decomposers, such as bacteria, break it down. Over time, even energy in the bones is cycled back into the environment.

Forming fossil fuel is not the only way carbon is tied up. Large amounts of carbon dioxide are dissolved in the oceans. Some marine organisms convert this carbon dioxide into calcium carbonate for their shells. When these organisms die, their shells fall to the bottom of the ocean. In some oceans, chemical processes cause carbon dioxide dissolved in ocean water to form calcium carbonate and precipitate, or separate out. Given enough time, the shells and calcium carbonate build up and turn into limestone. This process may tie up carbon for millions of years. Later, erosion slowly releases this carbon back into the environment.

The carbon cycle is a delicate balance between carbon in the atmosphere and carbon that is tied up in organisms or the environment. This balance is altered when fossil fuels are burned. Exactly how this will affect the balance remains a subject that is debated among scientists.

Water, nitrogen, and phosphorus all cycle through the environment in similar ways. Each has its own specific way of cycling, but they are all just as important.

Chapter Three

Communities

Acommunity is a collection of populations that interact with each other. All the populations live in the same area and under the same conditions. All of the organisms are adapted to the conditions in the area in which they live. When the conditions in the area change, the organisms must change, too.

CHANGES AND THE ENVIRONMENT

Ecosystems are constantly changing. Some changes take place quickly and some take place very slowly. The changes in the ecosystem affect the communities of organisms that live there. When ecologists study these changes, they often find patterns that further our understanding of how ecosystems develop and change. These patterns often help ecologists understand how an ecosystem will respond to rapid changes that disrupt it.

Changes in the ecosystem affect the organisms living there by affecting environmental factors such as temperature, water abundance, or food availability. Whenever a change in the ecosystem causes a change in a factor that affects an organism's ability to survive, it is called a limiting factor. A limiting factor is a biotic or abiotic factor that restricts the numbers, lives, reproduction, or distribution of organisms.

Organisms are able to tolerate some change in their environment. For example, some plants need warm and sunny conditions most of the time, with a steady supply of water to allow the plants to grow well and produce lots of seeds. If the

POPULATION/SALT CONCENTRATION LINE GRAPH

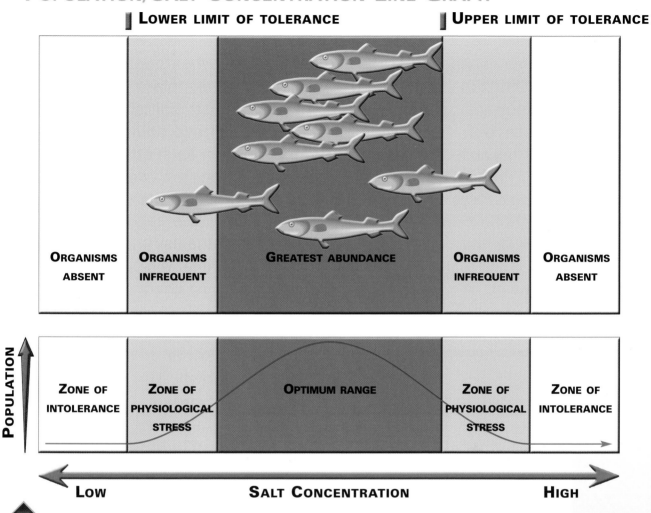

LOWER LIMIT OF TOLERANCE　　**UPPER LIMIT OF TOLERANCE**

| ORGANISMS ABSENT | ORGANISMS INFREQUENT | GREATEST ABUNDANCE | ORGANISMS INFREQUENT | ORGANISMS ABSENT |

POPULATION

| ZONE OF INTOLERANCE | ZONE OF PHYSIOLOGICAL STRESS | OPTIMUM RANGE | ZONE OF PHYSIOLOGICAL STRESS | ZONE OF INTOLERANCE |

LOW　　**SALT CONCENTRATION**　　**HIGH**

Line graphs illustrate a value that is based on two variables, which are represented by a horizontal line and a vertical line. This line graph shows that the population of certain types of fish depends on the salt concentration in their water. Too much salt in the water is just as harmful as too little. As you can see in the diagram, if the salt concentration is too low or too high, organisms are absent.

weather during the growing season is too cloudy, too wet, or too dry, the plant will survive but will not produce as many seeds. The ability of an organism to withstand variations in the environment is called tolerance. Some organisms can tolerate great changes in their environment while others cannot tolerate change well at all.

SUCCESSION

Some changes in ecosystems take place when populations grow or shrink in size. Some of these changes take place in an orderly, natural way within a community. Ecologists call these changes succession. Succession affects both plant and animal communities because the two are interdependent on each other.

Primary succession takes place when, for example, something causes a broad area of new rock surface to be exposed. This might be caused by a lava flow or the retreat of a continental glacier. At first, no plants or animals are found in the area. Over time, wind and water deposit small bits of rock in depressions or cracks.

SUCCESSION TIMELINE

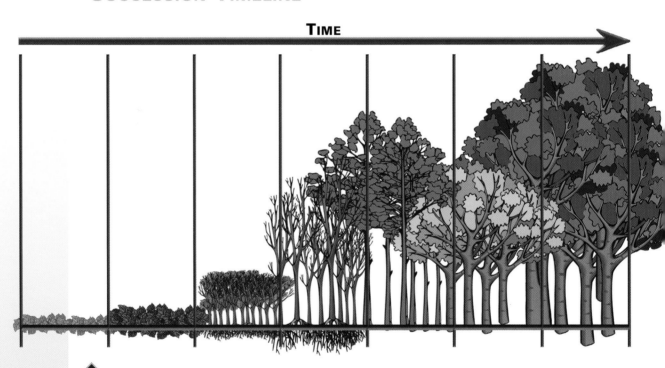

TIME

Timelines list events in chronological order. In this succession timeline, we see the process of a forest reaching maturity. On the left, the timeline begins with small plants. Finally, on the right of the timeline, the forest is mature and hardwood trees dominate.

This is just enough for the first plants to take root. These first plants are called pioneer species. Pioneer species are usually lichens or mosses. These plants attract animals that can feed off of them. Over time, waste from the animals and decaying matter from the plants create thin pockets of soil.

The thin pockets of soil are enough to support grasses. As these live, the grasses attract more animals and they create more soil. In time, enough soil exists to support shrubs. As the soils increase in depth and quality, larger shrubs begin growing. Eventually, softwood trees begin growing. Then, with enough time, hardwood tree species begin replacing the softwood trees. Finally, a hardwood forest covers the area. Throughout the process, the different communities attract different kinds of animals. Different insects, reptiles, birds, and mammals are parts of the different communities. When the area reaches the hardwood forest stage, the community becomes stable and undergoes little or no change. This is called a climax community.

Succession does not always follow a steady increase. Sometimes succession moves rapidly at some stages and very slowly in others. Succession can also have setbacks that cause it to start over. For example, a forest fire can burn through a forest and kill all the trees. Succession will restart almost immediately. With plenty of soil present, grasses, weeds, and flowers will begin sprouting. Shrubs and trees will begin sprouting from seeds. In just a matter of a several years, trees will begin growing above the fast-growing shrubs. Animals will be attracted back to the area by the plants and new communities. In tens of years, the area will be forested again, but will not necessarily be a climax community. Ecologists call this process secondary succession.

BIOMES

Geographic areas where similar plant and animal climax communities exist are grouped together into biomes. A biome is a large group of ecosystems, which share the same type of climax community. A

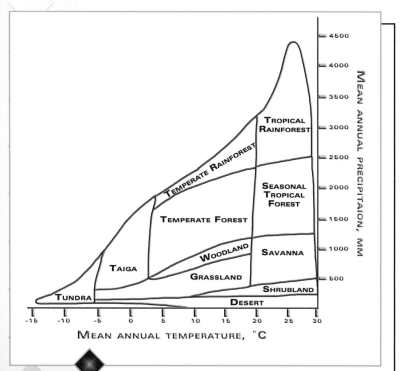

MEAN ANNUAL PRECIPITAION, MM

TROPICAL RAINFOREST

TEMPERATE RAINFOREST

TEMPERATE FOREST

SEASONAL TROPICAL FOREST

WOODLAND

SAVANNA

TAIGA

GRASSLAND

SHRUBLAND

TUNDRA

DESERT

MEAN ANNUAL TEMPERATURE, °C

The mean annual temperature and the mean annual rainfall determine which biomes are present. This chart shows the relationship between temperature and rainfall for each different type of biome.

biome is not a specific place. For example, a tropical rain forest biome is not one particular place. Instead, a tropical rain forest is any place where similar conditions, plants, and animals are present. Biomes may also be defined by two abiotic environmental factors—rainfall and temperature. These two environmental factors are a strong force in determining which plants and animals may live in a geographic area.

AQUATIC BIOMES

Aquatic biomes are those that exist in the water. They may be in either fresh or salt water. Saltwater or marine biomes include a wide variety of communities, such as coral reefs, open ocean, deep ocean, polar ice, estuaries, and intertidal areas. Freshwater biomes include rivers, streams, lakes, ponds, and wetlands such as marshes and swamps.

Aquatic biomes are incredibly varied in their makeup. Terrestrial or land biomes also vary widely in their conditions. Tropical biomes are those found near the equator. Tropical biomes have high temperatures year-round and often have heavy, seasonal rainfall. Tropical biomes never have temperatures below freezing. The temperature difference between summer and winter is usually very small. Because of the warm temperatures and abundant rainfall, communities in tropical biomes tend to have a wide variety of plant and animals species living together.

TEMPERATE BIOMES

Temperate biomes are those found in midlatitude environments, such as those in much of the United States and Europe. Temperate biomes have more variation in temperature than tropical biomes. Temperate biomes have a winter season that is much cooler than the summer season. As a result, some trees lose their leaves in the fall. Rainfall tends to be less than that in tropical biomes. Communities in temperate biomes are made up of a variety of species of plants and animals, but the numbers are nowhere near those found in tropical biomes.

In desert biomes, plants are widely scattered. Most of these plants have thorns or sharp leaves to keep animals from eating them.

DESERT BIOMES

Desert biomes are hot, dry regions with low humidity. Desert biomes often have a big temperature difference between daytime high and nighttime low temperatures as well as very hot summers and cold winters. Rainfall amounts are low and most rain falls quickly during storms. Communities in desert biomes have a good variety of plants and animals. To survive in desert biomes, communities are adapted to wide temperature changes and receiving little water.

GRASSLAND BIOMES

Grassland biomes are often called plains, steppes, savannas, prairies, or pampas depending on where they are located. The communities found in grassland biomes have grasses as their

BIOME MAP

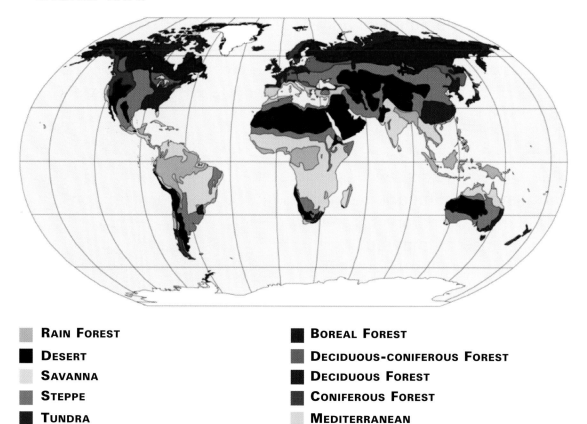

	RAIN FOREST		BOREAL FOREST
	DESERT		DECIDUOUS-CONIFEROUS FOREST
	SAVANNA		DECIDUOUS FOREST
	STEPPE		CONIFEROUS FOREST
	TUNDRA		MEDITERRANEAN

We use maps all the time, but most people don't realize that they are graphic organizers. Maps illustrate a location of any type. This map shows where biomes are distributed around the world.

main type of vegetation. Grasslands are usually flat or have gently rolling hills. Temperatures in the summer are usually warm to hot, and winter temperatures are mild to very cold. The moderate rainfall is seasonal with a distinct wet and dry season. In the past, grassland communities often had large herds of grazing animals living on them. Today, grasslands have been transformed into areas for growing crops, such as wheat, and for grazing cattle.

Closer to the poles are large communities dominated by coniferous forests. The dominant trees are fir, spruce, and pine trees. These communities make up a biome called taiga. Taiga biomes usually have mild summers and very cold winters with moderate amounts of precipitation. Animals in these communities often survive the harsh winters by hibernating or migrating to warmer climates.

TUNDRA BIOMES

Tundra biomes are found close to the North Pole or on high mountaintops. Tundra biomes have mild temperatures during the summer and very cold winter temperatures. Precipitation is usually low and may be just slightly more than deserts receive. Arctic tundra is found in the very high northern latitudes near the North Pole. The soil here is frozen during the winter and only the surface thaws during the summer. Below the surface, the soil is frozen year-round. This permanently frozen soil is called permafrost. When the surface of the soil thaws, abundant water is available and the soil is waterlogged. Plant communities that survive have shallow roots. Common plants are grasses, sedges, rushes, small woody shrubs, mosses, and lichens. Most animals that live here migrate to these areas during the summer to feed, and then leave in the winter. Alpine tundra is found on high mountaintops. It is similar to arctic tundra except that the soil is usually not waterlogged.

Biomes are a useful way of classifying the characteristics of communities. A temperate biome in Europe will have similar conditions as a temperate biome in North America. While both biomes will have different species of animals and plants there, the roles of these plants and animals will be similar. This makes studying and understanding the interdependence of the plants, animals, and the environment much easier.

CHAPTER FOUR

POPULATIONS

When most people hear the term "population," they immediately think of the number of people who live in a city or the number of people who live on Earth. To an ecologist, the term has a very specialized meaning. A population is a group of organisms of a single species that lives and interbreeds in the same location at the same time. Populations change over time by growing or shrinking. Sometimes these changes are caused by natural factors, sometimes not.

HOW POPULATIONS GROW

When a population grows, it sometimes follows a type of growth described as exponential growth. Exponential growth occurs when the population grows at an ever-increasing rate. Mathematically, exponential growth occurs when a population grows at a rate proportional to its size. Most people understand exponential growth as extremely fast growth. On a chart, the line indicating growth curves up rather than being straight. Exponential growth leads to a population explosion. When graphed, exponential growth creates a J-shaped curve.

A population cannot continue to grow exponentially. At some point in the population's growth, some factor limits further growth. This limiting factor may be either a biotic or abiotic factor in the environment. Abiotic factors that limit growth could be available food or space of the population. The largest population size that can be achieved because of the limiting factor is called

J-SHAPED GRAPH

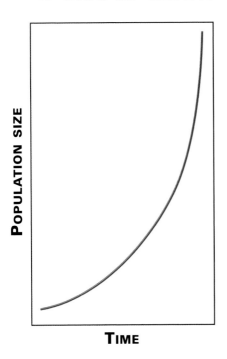

POPULATION SIZE

TIME

S-SHAPED GRAPH

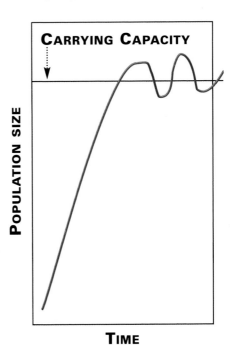

CARRYING CAPACITY

POPULATION SIZE

TIME

With line graphs, we can see a value based on two different factors. Here, the J-shaped line graph shows exponential population growth. The S-shaped line graph shows what happens when some limiting factor (the carrying capacity) is reached by a population.

the carrying capacity. Ecologists often represent carrying capacity with the letter K.

A graph showing population growth is usually described as an S-shaped graph. The population grows exponentially up to the carrying capacity and then levels off. When the population exceeds the carrying capacity, the limiting factor causes the death rate to exceed the birth rate until population returns to the carrying capacity. When the population is below the carrying capacity, the limiting factor does not affect the population, and the birth rate exceeds the death rate until the population returns to the carrying capacity. These trends are seen on a graph as the fluctuations above and below the carrying capacity.

Patterns of Population Growth

These two models accurately describe what really happens as populations grow. However, in nature, most populations are already more or less in equilibrium with other populations within a community. Populations usually follow one of two different growth patterns.

The first growth pattern is rapid growth. Fish offer a good example of this growth pattern. Fish reproduce quickly and have many offspring in a short period of time. Fish have a very short life span and their populations can increase quickly in a short amount of time. The other growth pattern is a slow growth. Whales provide

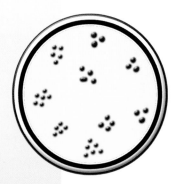

This school of fish shows members of the same species. Fish reproduce quickly and have rapid population growth.

Sequence-of-Events Diagram

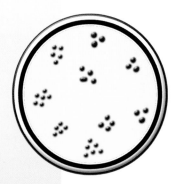 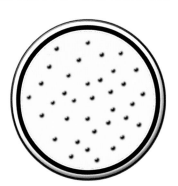 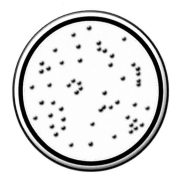

A sequence-of-events diagram illustrates how something changes over time. This diagram reveals that populations move from clumped, to evenly spaced, to random dispersion over time.

an example of this type of growth pattern. Whales live for a very long time and they have only a few offspring during their lives. The offspring take many years before they reach the age when they can have offspring. This causes the population of whales to grow very slowly over a long period of time.

Each of these growth patterns has advantages based on the environmental conditions. A fly population, for example, is able to grow quickly to take advantage of favorable environmental conditions. Flies tend to live in rapidly changing environmental conditions and must be able to take advantage of times when conditions are best for reproduction. Whales are best suited for living in an environment that does not change rapidly. Their slow but steady growth rate does not deplete their food supplies because the food supply is available at a steady rate.

INTERACTIONS AMONG POPULATIONS AND THE ENVIRONMENT

Populations are described by three key characteristics. These are population size, population density, and population dispersion. Population size refers to the number of individuals in a population. Population density refers to the number of individuals in a certain area. Population dispersion describes how a population spreads out across the area where it lives.

The size of populations may also be affected by competition from within or outside the population. Competition occurs when organisms try to use the same resource. The resource may be food, water, nest sites, or any other factor. If the resource is limited, the organisms must try to obtain the resource more efficiently than other organisms. Competition for the same resource is reduced when each population becomes specialized to use only part of a resource or to use resources at different times from other populations. When an organism uses a resource in a specialized manner, this is defined as the organism's niche. A niche is the particular role an organism plays in the environment regarding how it feeds, reproduces, and lives, and how it interacts with the abiotic factors.

Interactions between populations may also affect both their sizes. This type of interaction is seen in predator-prey relationships. The predator is the animal that eats another animal, called the prey. The most well-known example of predator-prey interactions is between the lynx, a type of cat, and the hare, or rabbit.

The data in the chart came from records of the Hudson's Bay Company, one of the first corporations in North America, which controlled the fur trade in Canada. Trappers would trap lynxes and hares and sell the fur to the company. The company records of the number of furs sold in a year reflect the sizes of the two populations. Lynxes are a predator that feed on hares, its prey. On the

POPULATION/TIME LINE GRAPH

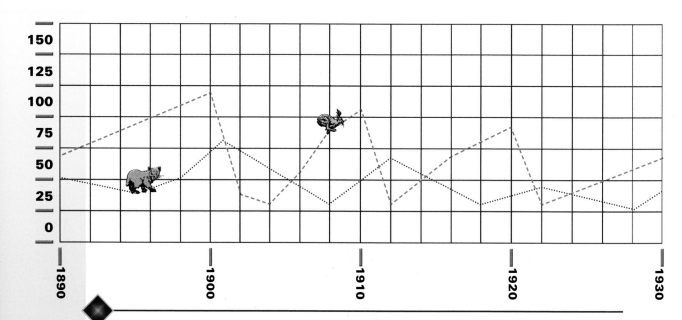

Line graphs illustrate any number of values depending on the variables that they're based on. This line graph shows how the populations of lynxes and rabbits fluctuated over a period of time. One population decreased while the other population increased.

chart, you can clearly see that the two populations follow a cycle. When hare populations are high, lynx populations are low.

Limiting factors that affect population size may be either biotic or abiotic. These limiting factors may regulate the available food or water, temperature, or space. Sometimes the limiting factor can change, which causes a change in the carrying capacity. For example, a drought may reduce the amount of food available and lower the carrying capacity. The population would respond to the lower carrying capacity by reducing in size. Conversely, several wetter-than-normal years could increase the carrying

IDEA RAKE

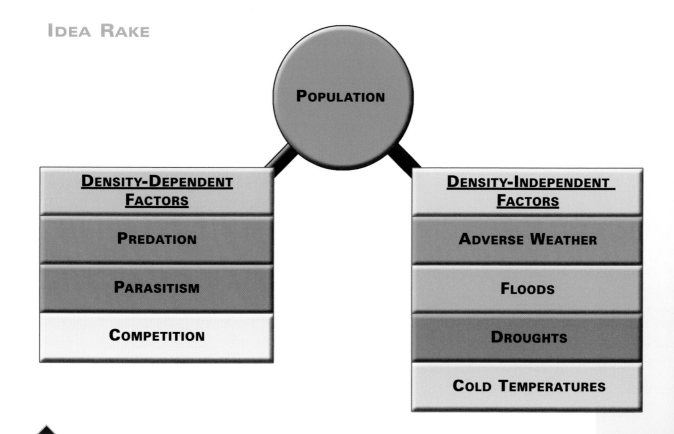

Idea rakes are graphic organizers that are useful for helping us break apart a concept into its component parts. This idea rake shows that population size depends on two sets of factors: density-dependent factors and density-independent factors.

capacity resulting in an increase in population size. The limiting factors that affect carrying capacity can be categorized as either density-dependent factors or density-independent factors.

Density-dependent factors are ones that affect a population based on how closely together the organisms live. Disease is a density-dependent factor. If a population lives close together and its members have frequent contact, a disease may spread rapidly through the population. If the population is spread out and members of the population seldom meet, a disease most likely will not spread through the population.

Density-independent factors will affect a population regardless of the population density. Big storms, floods, or droughts are examples of density-independent factors. Regardless of the contact between members of a population, these factors will affect all members of the population.

As the human population grows, it takes more space. We build cities and roads. This action takes away habitats where entire communities of organisms existed before. We change grasslands into areas for grazing cattle and farms for growing crops. To increase the production on farms and ranches, pesticides and other methods are used to kill the organisms that compete with or eat cattle or crops. Human wastes pollute the land, air, and water. This also affects all other animals and plants.

Waste disposal is also a problem with population growth. As the human population grows, the amount of wastes generated increases, too. The average American throws away about twenty-six pounds (twelve kilograms) of trash a week. Most of this trash ends up in landfills.

Of all the species, humans have the greatest impact on the environment, plants, and other animals. This is because humans create the most harmful waste.

GLOBAL ENVIRONMENTAL CHANGES FROM HUMAN IMPACT

Humans have clearly been able to affect populations and communities wherever human activity is concentrated. However, there

HUMAN POPULATION GROWTH CHART

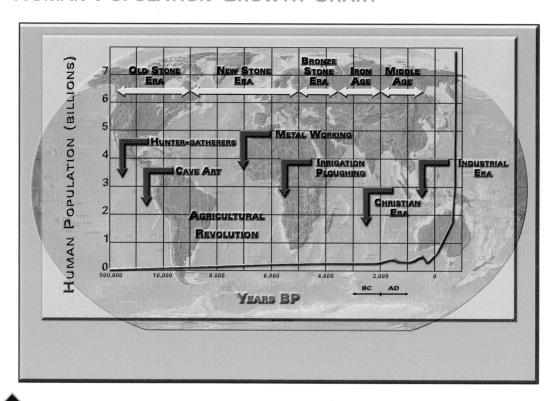

Growth charts allow us to track the rate and amount of growth of something over a period of time. This human population growth chart shows that the human population began to grow rapidly beginning just several hundred years ago. This was due, in part, to the technological advances made during the Industrial Era.

have been some human activities that affect the environment of the entire planet.

Global warming is a rise in the planet's average temperature. Whether global warming is occurring and what causes it are both controversial subjects. What is known is that Earth stays warm because of the greenhouse effect. The greenhouse effect is Earth's natural heating process. Some gases, such as carbon dioxide, allow heat energy from the sun to enter Earth's atmosphere, but prevent it from escaping. This traps heat energy in the atmosphere and warms the planet. If you have ever gotten into a car with all the windows rolled up on a sunny day, you know that the interior of the car is much warmer than the exterior. The greenhouse effect works the same way. In the car, heat energy passes through the windows, but the windows prevent that heat energy from escaping.

TEMPERATURE/TIME GRAPH

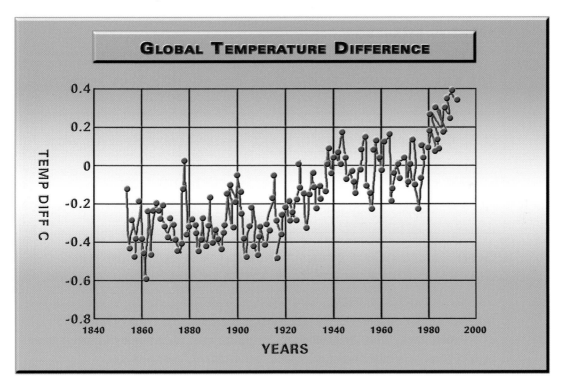

Temperature/time graphs are a form of line graph that allow us to see how the average temperature of an area changes over time. The information these graphs give us allows us to track climate change. This temperature/time graph provides evidence that supports the theory of global warming.

Environmentalist Events Timeline

1852	**The United States imports sparrows from Germany to protect crops from caterpillars.**
1854	**Henry David Thoreau writes *Walden: or, Life in the Woods*, and asserts people should live in harmony with nature.**
1872	**Yellowstone becomes a national park.**
1914	**Last passenger pigeon dies in captivity.**
1962	**Rachel Carson writes *Silent Spring* and describes the negative effects of pesticides.**
1970	**The Environmental Protection Agency (EPA) is formed.**
1973	**U.S. Congress establishes the Endangered Species Act.**
1990	**U.S. tuna processors stop accepting tuna caught in nets that also trap dolphins.**
1996	**Glen Canyon Dam opens to simulate a flood on the Colorado River to try to restore habitats downstream.**
2001	**National Aeronautics and Space Administration (NASA) confirms that the growing season in the Northern Hemisphere is getting longer, possibly due to global warming.**

Event timelines provide detailed descriptions of important occurrences in a particular subject. These descriptions are listed in chronological order, which allows us to track the events through history. Using this environmentalist events timeline, we can see the important steps that environmentalists have taken over the years to preserve nature.

The carbon dioxide levels in Earth's atmosphere have been steadily rising since the mid-1800s. Scientists also predict that global warming may affect rainfall patterns. Some areas will become too warm or too dry for agriculture while other areas may become warm enough and wet enough for agriculture. This will cause shifts not

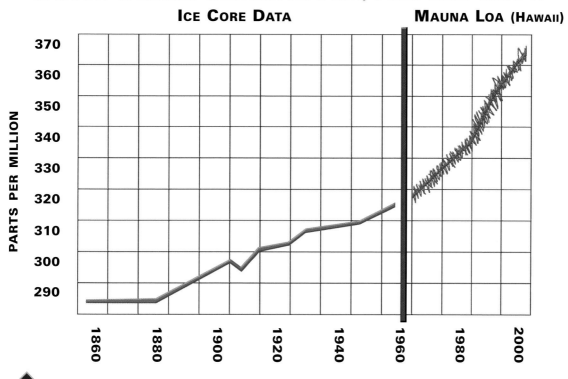

CARBON DIOXIDE CONCENTRATION/TIME LINE GRAPH

ICE CORE DATA   MAUNA LOA (HAWAII)

Line graphs allow us to measure a certain quantity based on two specific factors. This carbon dioxide concentration/time graph shows us that carbon dioxide is increasing in the atmosphere over time. The measurements were taken first from air bubbles in glacier ice cores and then from Hawaii's Mauna Loa Observatory.

only in agriculture but also within Earth's biomes. Depending on the rate at which this occurs, plants and animals may not adapt well to the changes. Because of the interdependence of all plant and animals within the environment, any changes that take place will affect all organisms on Earth.

GLOSSARY

abiotic Relating to nonliving factors in the environment, such as air, water, and light.

autotrophs Organisms that produce their own food.

biosphere The part of Earth where life is found. It extends high into the atmosphere, deep underground, and to the depths of the oceans.

biotic Relating to living factors in the environment, such as plants and animals.

carnivore An animal that eats only meat.

carrying capacity The largest population that an ecosystem can support over a long period of time.

commensalism A relationship between two organisms in which one benefits and the other is neither helped nor harmed.

community All the organisms that live in an ecosystem.

consumers Organisms that must eat other organisms for food.

decomposer Organisms that break down dead plant or animal matter.

density-dependent Relating to factors affecting life, such as disease, that depend on having all members of a population in close contact.

density-independent Relating to factors affecting life, such as drought, that affect all members of a population regardless of whether they have close contact.

ecology The branch of science that studies the interdependence of plants, animals, and the environment.

ecosystem A self-sustaining collection of populations and their environment.

exponential growth Explosive population growth where the number of individual increases at an ever-increasing rate.

food chain A possible route for matter and energy to pass through an ecosystem.

food web All the possible routes for matter and energy to pass through an ecosystem.

global warming An increase in the average global temperature.

greenhouse effect The ability of the atmosphere to trap heat by allowing it to enter but not escape.

herbivore An animal that eats only plants.

limiting factor Anything that limits the survival of organisms.

mutualism A relationship between two organisms in which both benefit from the relationship.

omnivore An animal that eats both plants and meat.

parasitism A relationship in which one organism benefits at the expense of the other organism.

population All members of the same species living and reproducing in the same geographic area at the same time.

producers Organisms, such as plants, that produce their own energy.

scavenger An animal that eats recently deceased animals.

succession The natural and orderly progress of different communities over a period of time.

symbiosis A close association between two organisms of different species.

FOR MORE INFORMATION

Environmental Protection Agency
Ariel Rios Building
1200 Pennsylvania Avenue, N.W.
Washington, DC 20460
(202) 272-0167
http://www.epa.gov

National Wildlife Federation
11100 Wildlife Center Drive
Reston, VA 20190-5362
(800) 822-9919
http://www.nwf.org

WEB SITES

Due to the changing nature of Internet links, the Rosen Publishing Group, Inc., has developed an online list of Web sites related to the subject of this book. This site is updated regularly. Please use this link to access the list:

http://www.rosenlinks.com/ugosle/ingo

FOR FURTHER READING

Ball, Jackie, and Anna Prokos. *Ecology* (Discovery Channel School Science). Milwaukee, WI: Gareth Stevens Publishing, 2004.

Berger, Melvin, and Gilda Berger. *Life in a Rainforest.* Philadelphia, PA: Chelsea House Publishers, 1998.

Jennings, Terry. *Ecology: The Study of Living Things* (Investigating Science). Milwaukee, WI: Gareth Stevens Publishing, 2002.

Kudlinski, Kathleen, and Ted Lewin. *Rachel Carson: Pioneer of Ecology* (Women of Our Time). Reissue ed. London, England: Puffin Books, 1997.

MacMillan, Dianne M. *Life in a Deciduous Forest*. Minneapolis, MN: Lerner Publications, 2003.

National Geographic. *Ecology*. New York, NY: Glencoe/ McGraw-Hill, 2002.

Patent, Dorothy Hinshaw. *Life in a Desert*. Minneapolis, MN: Lerner Publications, 2003.

Stewart, Melissa. *Life in a Wetland*. Minneapolis, MN: Lerner Publications, 2003.

BIBLIOGRAPHY

Begon, Michael, et al. *Population Ecology: A Unified Study of Animals and Plants*. Malden, MA: Blackwell Publishing, 1996.

Dawson, John. *The Nature of Plants: Habitats, Challenges, and Adaptations*. Portland, OR: Timber Press, 2005.

Glantz, Micheal H. *Climate Affairs: A Primer*. Washington, DC: Island Press, 2003.

Gotelli, Nicholas J. *A Primer of Ecology*. Sunderland, MA: Sinauer Associates, 2001.

Miller, Gary, and Robert E. Ricklefs. *Ecology*, Fourth ed. New York, NY: W. H. Freeman, 1999.

Morin, Peter J. *Community Ecology*. Malden, MA: Blackwell Publishing, 1999.

ABOUT THE AUTHOR

Allan B. Cobb is a science writer living in central Texas. He has a degree in aquatic biology and has worked in the environmental field as a biologist and chemist. He has also collected numerous new species of animals in caves in North and Central America.

PHOTO CREDITS

Cover, p. 1, 4–5, 7, 10, 11, 12, 13, 16, 17, 27 © Royalty-Free/Nova Development Corporation; graphics pp. 8, 9, 18, 20, 23, 24, 26, 28, 31, 32 (bottom), 34, 35, 38, 39, 40, 41 courtesy of Nelson Sá; p. 21 © Alan & Sandy Carey/Zefa/Corbis; p. 32 (top) © Stephen Frink/Corbis; p. 37 © Alan Schein Photography/Corbis.

Designer: Nelson Sá; Editor: Nicholas Croce; Photo Researcher: Nelson Sá